BY WAY OF DUST AND RAIN

MARK FITZGERALD

Cinnamon Press
:: small miracles from distinctive voices ::

Published by Cinnamon Press
Meirion House
Tanygrisiau
Blaenau Ffestiniog
Gwynedd, LL41 3SU
www.cinnamonpress.com

The right of Mark Fitzgerald to be identified as author of this work has been asserted by him in accordance with the Copyright, Designs and Patent Act, 1988. Copyright © 2010, 2019 (2nd edition) Mark Fitzgerald.
ISBN: 978-1-78864-064-0

British Library Cataloguing in Publication Data. A CIP record for this book can be obtained from the British Library.
All rights reserved. No part of this publication may be reproduced, stored in a retrieval system, or transmitted in any form or by any means, electronic, mechanical, photocopying, recording or otherwise without the prior written permission of the publishers. This book may not be lent, hired out, resold or otherwise disposed of by way of trade in any form of binding or cover other than that in which it is published, without the prior consent of the publishers.

Designed and typeset in Palatino by Cinnamon Press. Printed in Poland. Cover design by Adam Craig.
Cinnamon Press is represented in the UK by Inpress Ltd and in Wales by the Welsh Books Council.

Acknowledgements

The author gratefully acknowledges the editors of the following publications where some of these poems previously appeared: *Beltway Poetry Quarterly, Crab Creek Review, Freefall, Out of Chaos, Parting Gifts, Poetry Midwest, Poetry Motel, Squaw Review, Temenos* and *5th gear*. Poems in this collection have also been featured in anthologies, including *Only Connect* (Cinnamon Press) and *3LIGHTS Gallery* (Wilkinson). Sincerest thanks to Eric Pankey, Joan Houlihan and Robert Hass for their wisdom, kind words and encouragement. I am also grateful to Jan Fortune for believing in these poems. Special thanks to Andy Fogle for reading this manuscript and offering suggestions to improve it. And my deepest gratitude to Sara Paige Shepherd for all her love and support.

Mark Fitzgerald is also the author of *Downburst,* Cinnamon Press. His poetry has appeared in various periodicals, including *Santa Clara Review, Slipstream, Crab Creek Review, Naugatuck River Review* and *Beltway Poetry Quarterly.* His work has also appeared in two anthologies by unbound CONTENT, *Scratching Against the Fabric* and *What Lies Beyond the Frame.* Mark teaches writing and literature at the University of Maryland and was recently awarded a writing fellowship from the Virginia Center for the Creative Arts. He lives in Oakton, Virginia with his wife, Paige, and son, Blake.

Contents

Inviting the Invisible
Disintegration   11
Carousel   12
Quartet   14
Built to Code   15
White Sweater   16
Naming Olives in Saint-Rèmy   18
Château Marmont: Take 2   19
Inviting the Invisible   20
Big-Rig through Stolen Night   21
Distracting the Rain in Le Père Lachaise
    Amid Ash & Halo   22
    Stoned Immaculate (1943–1971)   24
    All that is Not You (1876–1933)   25
    Intriguing the Moss (1871–1922)   26
    Outcasts Always Mourn (1854–1900)   27
    With a Wayward Crystal Kite (1859–1891)   28
    Impromptu in P Minor (1810–1849)   29

Clawing at Bark
This Just In   33
Back at His Desk   34
Jujubes   35
Climatic Oscillation   36
Hunger   37
Urban Stardust   38
Reciprocity   39
Against Wasps   40
Clawing at Bark
    Tigris Balica   42
    Tigris Sondaica   43
    Tigris Virgata   44
Pinnacle   45

Off Camera
- Venetian Mask 49
- Millennium Retribution in Key West 50
- Consolation 52
- Nocturne with a Dash of Oblivion 53
- Third Law of Moxie 54
- Moratorium 56
- Snow & Branches 58
- Potomac at Last Light First 59
- Espresso at Villa Cimbrone 60
- Raking Leaves 61
- As Twilight Winks 62
- Off Camera 64

for Paige

By Way of Dust and Rain

Inviting the Invisible

Disintegration

The ladder by the side
of the house has rusted, the garden's
gone to wilderness. There is no way
through the mesh where dreams
tumble tangled below
the radar: the work too exhausted,
the potential too transfigured, swept
across empty yards like leaves
before a storm.
                The staked plots, endless
halls, splashing of paint, the hired hands
follow veering tracks of restlessness
and vanish.
            What belongs?
The bustle is barely noticeable
in the hanging stillness of the drying
lines, with the steel clock mainstreamed
and set to go.
              Yet your decision
was made long before the lesson
of the hyacinth, before tunnels
fell: rock against incessant
rock. Was it for this you lost
your footprints to the blue wave
bursting before the stairs? And now
those hours sipping tea advance
on death like a steamer
headed to port?
              Let the city's hum
meet the country's hush. Even stones
fall apart. Take me
to the canyons, to the stories
and silences beneath
a thin moon soon to be forgotten.

Carousel

She wants the white horse, the one
prancing with its head bowed
in the center ring. Not the leaping
kangaroo, or ostrich with its giant
plume and gaunt neck. The one
with the emerald saddle and brass
buckles at ease among the menagerie.
Because this is how we first
set out: wistful children thin and round,
eyes like glass, like stolen rubies.
She sees no other, will go no
other way. Counter clockwise,
as the clouds push east, she canters
through bay air, as the tide fades,
as The Blue Danube—tremolo, scherzo—
pipes on. No matter the stirrups
are too long: soon they'll be too
short. Soon the martingale
will go slack between the barberries.
And if she could do it again? Lasso
the legend, a bright-dark hilltop
where a grave of sticks once stood
like grief in a hut—do you think
she'd chase the rabbit? The one
with the fancy whiskers and prim
tail? What then would she say
to her mother about the dying orchard?
Her lover in charge of the stables?

White horse—colt of cactus and star,
storybook and violin, threshing field,
charger, hearse—gallop us past sly
sprawling squalls to summer in the valley
where an orange ring of poppies glazing
the hillside floats like hope
at a fair, sharpens the pale hunger of dusk.

Quartet

Cold square. Steel morning.
Tower bells repeat as leaves
drop to amber grass.

A crow soars past a
ramshackle barn just before
the scraping of plows.

Tulips inverted
from moonlight: checkered anchors
in a quiet pond.

The stench of king crabs
drifts in salt air. Caterwaul.
Hot sand. Razor shells.

Built to Code

For all its stark geometry the blinds
suppress a tenderness. The stairs are where
you put them, but less than what was climbed.
Refuge rescued from remorse, these walls tore
down trees, the majesty of natural
canopy, the blue jay's perch. It will take
time to bring the outside in, unravel
the carpets, brighten walls, finish the deck.
Time to avoid the neighbors. And why not
a pergola above the front entrance?
A roof garden over the garage? What
do you surmise? A fence? Why, yes, a fence
replete with recrimination, a gate
before beds of black-eyed Susans, your gaze.

White Sweater

for Paige

The storm absorbed us, but we blamed
   it on the work. The wheel
we pushed turned against us. The wind
   drove us out the door, blew
back our questions for some
   other day. But one day at a time
makes many days and often
   the distance between being
and knowing finds us
   rocking in darkness at the edge
of the porch.
              I went away for awhile, fell
into a group of martyrs: downtrodden
   creatures merely trying
to survive. Maybe it was just a place
   to be—Munich in the rain. I stood
listening under a vacant tarp
   while the drumming seeped
into continuance, while loss, taking
   stock of itself, grew ardent. The sky
became a scarlet cavern and I closed
   my eyes and traced
the answer I'd been trying
   to outlive.

       Maybe I came back
the night I caught you sewing
   that old sweater you love—softer
now, but not as white. Piecing it
   back, finding the weave. The way
memory has a weave. The way
   the candlelight brushes your face,
or fruition, when you least
   expect it, creeps up and becomes
everything you see, as though
   the world is thinking with you.

Naming Olives in Saint-Rèmy

The sparrows gulp the splintered light,
flee the grove in crazed trajectories.

What drives brilliance to despair?
No one can know all that went on

here, but the trees seem less certain
than the ones Van Gogh immortalized

beneath a yellow sky. What an odd thing
the touch, the stroke of the brush, is,

he wrote to Theo. Strolling the grounds mid-
afternoon, I think of an easel set in the sun,

turpentine in the throat, symptom
and syndrome—olives. One works as best

one can, one fills one's canvas regardless,
he penned from a small, iron-barred room.

Maybe affliction has nothing to do with sorrow,
what was lost between self and portrait, wheat

and reaper. At the village market, I try to say
Lucque, Picholine, Niçoise. A woman smiles

knowingly, spoons them gently into cartons.
Van Gogh, even in his early somber stage, must've

understood a ghostly vessel. Sanctity between
object and expression: battered hands at a dark table.

I imagine him trudging half-broken down the road,
translating the landscape as though to become it.

Château Marmont: Take 2

of course back then
no one cared
about tomorrow and those tuxedo nights
swung gin jazzed
like a string of trumpets
scaling octaves by surprise,
sashaying will
to way across
the city's nectar,
tomorrow didn't care
back then
snug beyond the verve
of rampage,
wind assaulting the canopy,
moon in utter spin,
frothing up the hubbub
until the avalanche
zapped the pundit, broke
past the eyes
of staggering dawn—
when we stole back
through the garden
the palms went red,
the skeleton fronds flinched,
as though the tide
had warned the tinsel—wrong
to be so brash
amid the shamble
of a fable gone
kaput,
        but that's just how we rolled,
I tell you, how
we stood in the now
back then, back
when we were all that
and then some of course

Inviting the Invisible

I wear my best suit, but nobody seems to notice.

She has a look of harmony. Our eyes
meet briefly, but it doesn't feel
like sharing. She tells me
to stop searching for things that aren't
there. Nothing that is not there and the nothing
that is, I say, quoting Stevens.
                                      Absence is hard
to describe, especially in winter, but let's try
a northern star that traces the unsaid
to a patch of blackened snow along
a stretch of highway that once was a grave-
yard for the demented.
                                  This can be solitary
work, private, exclusive like the weather,
and sometimes there's nothing but nothing to feel.

Like necessity ... or speeding traffic over forgotten bones.

Big-Rig through Stolen Night

All night the truck trucks
through the desert, a scene
so familiar as to become
unseen, all 18-wheels
barreling across wasteland,
time sedated but still on
schedule, a look of abandonment
through the windshield, it's all
headlights and highway, cash
on delivery, dropping
off, picking up, all 50
tons of it, tier upon tier, rising
and falling with clammy
palms on the wheel, a dusty
boot to the pedal,
the passage of sleep
in motion—who is it who shakes
in the night, shakes
on the road, shakes through the weather?—
with gears cranking
forward, shifting
back, boxes strapped
to walls, the truck
knocking against darkness,
deflation, desertion,
until the driver
rolls down the window
and comes alive
to the smell of diesel
amid green pastures,
the first sign of light.

Distracting the Rain in Le Père Lachaise

I Amid Ash & Halo

The weather hangs thick among the dead,
as if paying homage to a season where time ticks
in secret—did we ever really know it? When

exactly? I can feel the rain in my bones. I am
becoming what I cannot see. Or perhaps

I'm skipping to a frequency less divided, one
that saunters the Avenue Transversale
and pauses as the first trace of darkness enters

the trees. Ancient in their silence, their limbs
console a gray, numb sky. Their roots inhale

the dead. I want to know what the trees know
about the spirits, this twilight. Want to taste
the rain, to hear through the wind the dead

pronounce their names as if said
for the first time—their names heard for the first time

while at last they are being named. What is death for?
I ask through the branches. Life? And who in the last
of the dusk can discern the infinite from an instant,

casket from cradle, wind from dancing leaves
or flags trembling at half-mast? Blade by blade, the grass

of the dead is beginning to speak. A halo of ash,
some three centuries wide, takes hold of the gates,
takes over the eyes of the owl. As a child, I'd sometimes

dream of being strangled by a silence only night
understood. I now remember how hard I fought to stay alive,

the screech that bolted me awake—how I was saved—after I died.

II Stoned Immaculate (1943–1971)

Mine came in trances, through
the forked tongues of lizards.
I declared myself king, turned tricks

like a clown. Death is not divine. Try
Valium, sleeping in the rain.

Blake must have been high: no palace,
wisdom, nothing. What more
do you seek? The papers were wrong:

I entered this forest long before
Paris. Still grooving, crooning, shooting

for the sun, though more in tune, I must say,
brother, with the moon. There is no other side,
MR. MOJO, no RISIN. Only highway, wayward

desert, murder. Did I tell you how night knifes
your throat like a bow across a cello?

Drugs and booze: that's all they leave
me—it's all too sober. Can't say I blame my thin raft
of rebels. Can't say I miss those riotous rapids.

But what if I said death, like water, seeks its own
enormity? What if I said my doors open on burning

stone? Even six feet under the backbeat floods
west. One of Piaf's, no doubt. Can you
catch it? How redemptive, how macabre.

Now if you'll excuse me, it's time I slipped
on my snakeskins, skipped on back to town.

Oh yeah: see that Anna . . . give her . . . tell her I love her.

III All that is Not You (1876–1933)

Amour? I never again would risk
that word, I swore. That bright-towered
city was always just out of reach: my ship

heaved ashore by a sea too dark to silence.
Yet I sparked a Paris that only Paris

could ignite. A princess crowned queen, I sealed
la belle époque with the toss of a glove. How long
have I waited to be summoned from the living?

I vowed never again to weather the heart,
yet how I've longed for its seasons. *Merci!*

You've carried me back to the wine
of Dionysus. His leopards
ready my chariot. Soon I will bathe

in the silver stream. But your question awaits,
yes? There is no answer, no — we live

many deaths before we die. I've buried
so many lives. To stop loving is suicide. How life
streams on after life is a better question. For we,

we have died already. Strange
you didn't notice, *mon cher*. Our souls need only

the treetops now — moonlight,
the rain. Proust will explain. He's made a deal
with the rain. Ask him about my time. Question

the silver stream the eddy the pebble the ripple
answer the blood that steers your sea. My chariot approaches.

Au revoir. I live, love again, mon cher! Leave again . . .

IV Intriguing the Moss (1871–1922)

My dear princess? What passion,
savoir faire. She emboldened the salon
with a style worth drinking to. But even

a queen should bow to the rain, to the moody
montage, the pulse of gravity betrayed. There is

no sanctuary, covenant of transcendence. I knew
all along flesh is but a crocus doting on a diamond,
that death, without subtlety, without grandeur, would

too soon hurl this gem through vagary's window,
shattering the vanity of reflection, snapping

deception's shackles, before submerging us at last
beneath the telescope—the bursting rain—
of who we are. Rake your fingers across my black

marble grave. Compose the *froideur*
of our eternity. Can you not procure a purer oasis

than the sun-swept grapes you once helped harvest—
pluck and crush—in the sultry autumn
of an oak-aged vintage nosed now as destiny?

Again and again we are hurled headlong into the swamp,
yet how keenly we imagined our parting while living.

Sought it like fruit in our studios, danced it to laughter
in the clutch of infirmity, shivered it to dream. Time
is the lonely, only difference between breath and breeze,

you and I amid the steeples. Take heed, my friend: release
yourself before you close, expire only to rapture. Thunder.

Wilde will cast it for you: scale lightening, unzip the sky.

V Outcasts Always Mourn (1854–1900)

Returned to earth, we dry
the rain, we
wait again to drink the sun.

Death? Your question
is a frozen ocean. What is life? I answer.

A second, I lived. No longer
than a shooting star—I lived once,
I sang. Held hostage by intemperance,

I was possessed by the splendor
of sorrow, a hard-won humility

that never flowered. One season, no time.
In the mirror of creation, love was all
that mattered. Living. There is no secret,

no time, one season. I dwell in paradox,
while my passion for debauchery over

and over devours me. I invented the best wine
of my age and the critics bought it
by the barrel. Even Proust was brought

to tears. My life, my art, do you know it?
A shooting star, no longer. Pity's long broken

urn . . . a caterpillar molting its eyes. Thank you
for the lily—it means a great deal. In my dreams,
you know, I tend the lilacs. An angel or two

takes notice, if I'm lucky. They only bloom if I cry—
and so I cry. And so . . . forgive me, my muse, for not unzip-

ping the sky. Seurat will, I'm sure. He's better than I at goodbye.

VI With a Wayward Crystal Kite (1859–1891)

I'm dotting your question as you point it,
clustering the occasion: streaming, teasing,
slanting the sun, sails, see I'm breaking

the breakers. Wilde might soar a gull
into this twilight, swim fate ashore—but death

is neither portrait nor landscape. A lady
leaps and ceases leaping. The crowd
claps, the horse gallops on. Life breathes

no opposite. So what if it rained on the tower
when you most needed the city to shimmer?

Nothing elusive is ever lost. That slow twirling fan
didn't have to mean much to mean everything. Why,
my mystic, must you insist on insisting in some

higher quickening? What if there is no plight
to pilot? Chiseler to spite? No more light

than most I once possessed, yet more than most I felt
the light—I was possessed. I rose from line to curve:
first gentleman, then clown. Stole a Sunday

to wheedle a waterbank, became a delirious circus,
no, a quinsy, they said. I died too young

for some, but *c'est la vie*. My work never finished
what it wanted me to be. Embrace the question:
that's what my chef d'oeuvre will inflect

with all the flecks of the spectrum. To see afresh, you must
first blank out the canvass. Go to Chopin. You must trace

the dance of your muse, color the harbor of its symphony.

VII Impromptu in P Minor (1810–1849)

And so you've returned to rise again, to leave
once more to fall. Tell me, my prince, what
will they chisel on your stone? Who will

compose your last sonata? My song skates
from brink to brink: past the fog-kept gargoyles

of impasse, over frozen, crisscrossed chasms,
under onslaught, through incandescent cathedrals
of fugue—how the rain thawed the junipers, how I slipped

down the blue-black fever of neurosis, my wind-
tousled Vistula, my Amandine. There is a fifth season

we scarcely notice: a breaking sky at odds with night,
bolts through the nimbus, Venus ablaze from the tower—
cinder, ash, wind—turmoil in the afterglow, the pendulum

stalled in the throat of dawn's exegesis. What is a body
but the rain's distraction? What is a heart but the sun

stirred to waltz? Mine was a requiem shipwrecked
between eminence and home. I played because it was how
I knew to pray. I played because love knew no other way.

I wish that flush off the Seine, anointing the alders,
was your quest—that salvation was merely a window

over an ancient square. But such wishes chime best just wishing.
The concert belongs to the collage of our obliquity—hooves
on the cobbles, silk gloves, a scent of lavender—to the counter-

point of coda: unscored, uncoded. Tell me, my prince,
are those tears on my ivories, or is that just the rain

serenading the dark over the catacombs of augury's exhortation?

Clawing at Bark

This Just In

The nation's population
is increasing by one person every
14 seconds. So the Census Bureau

says. Soon it will top 300 million.
Birth and death and immigration,
but no talk of the milkweed near

the spider's web, no word of the
the plovers, the stones worn
smooth by the river, currents

that wake us and keep us awake.
The patience of the clock hangs
like dust above a mine, above

exhausted shoulders and calloused
hands. The hammers ring out.
The chisels of expectation and mis-

direction incise like a bull
through damnation. Nothing has changed.
Meanwhile babies sally forth

from wombs, breaches recur at borders,
and every 12 seconds someone
stops beating and begins to stiffen.

Yet no sign of the locusts.

Back at His Desk

Another year already.
He jots down the latest numbers
with a blunted pencil. Was it five
percent or just three? The phone
rings, but he doesn't pick
up. A drag and click will do
for now. Coffee, the usual hazel-
nut blend, comes later, then
The Times: a digression
on alternative fuels, news
of another space mission, some
gunfire in the Bronx.
Must have been three,
he thinks, pausing by the water
cooler. Another year.
Clean-collared defenses
betray vacant faces
tick-tocking to the moan
of the radiator. The carpet trembles
with every step. Through
the window he sees
no difference in the trees.

Jujubes

Street fumes, tattered cardboard, mice scuttling,
        scratching again screeching again

I'll get up soon, swear I will,
        hacking my feet my head to bleed again

Keep on, start believing,
        gnawing my teeth into scraping of bones again

Tell myself, couldn't be better,
        coughing up gobs of lies again

Hell I could: ain't in prison, got a city,
        tugging me down to tearing like rags again

Good pair of socks, some jujubes,
        plucking my eyes for fear of sleep again

The moon, a rusty old sax to kill time
        again clutching again breathing

Climatic Oscillation

The doors converge, the numbers light up.
The lift ascends to piped arrangements, supple
notes oozing from pinholes. A woman
the fragrance of apricots gets on at the 3rd floor,
asks for the time. *I'm late,* she says, adjusting
her bra, her nails like amnesia in riptide,
her hair. She presses 29, reconsiders, then 37.
I try not to stare, think maybe light conversation,
some small talk might ease our confinement:
an anecdote, the weather, pervading chain stores,
mutating aphids, *El Niño* ... A bearded man,
failing to discern up from down, hops on
at the 11th, presses lobby. *Hot and getting
hotter,* he says, his eyes on the floor.
Retreating glaciers, fires, floods, climatic
oscillation, SMALL TALK, I try to focus.
Stay cool, he urges, taking leave on the next
floor instead. *We'll try,* I say before noticing
the woman is clicking her tongue to a dumbed-
down version of *The Girl from Ipanema.*
When she walks, she's like a samba
that swings so cool ... *Really is hot out there,*
I second after a few beats. She lowers her shades
and tilts her head my way. *It's not supposed
to be like this,* she whispers. Now the cage
is climbing faster than mercury: 15, 20, 25 ...
The weather, you mean? She puffs out her lips.
It's absolutely vicious, disgusting. I nod.
Yes, yes, it is, my voice sounds shaky, false.
We need to get ready for the voyage, she adds,
fiddling with her cell phone. *Voyage?* The word
is easier. She looks straight ahead, not at me ...

Her number lights up. *We need to colonize the moon.*

Hunger

It grows stronger the more we feed it,
thrives too often in the flesh, in the raw
pang of wanting. Not in the wolf gnawing

through the door, but in what keeps
the wolf at bay. The expectation. The scent
of grilled sausages on the street. The long

line at the gallery. Not the conjugal visit,
but the date scrawled on the prison wall.
The impending deal, the prelude. Not the monk's

transcendence, but his self-denial. A child's
dream, not a father's approval. It beats back
discontent. The pebble thrown to the lover's

window, not the serenade. The last ticket
for the first bus out. Attainment's delusion
and the art of attainment. The sun before it rises.

Urban Stardust

I came a great distance to feign
goodbye. Your gift appeared as you vanished
into midnight smog. Where did you go
with your fists stuffed in your
trench coat?   That slipshod bar on Wilson
Boulevard felt ripe enough for a last hurrah
sans new memories. You wanted to tell
me something—or was it I who tried
to speak?—as the jukebox segued
into a folk ensemble that skewed
our jaws so cleverly. *I am going
slowly blind*, someone bellowed from behind
a wall of shoulders. What did we talk
about before you cracked your knuckles
and downed your double scotch?
We left without explanation, left
with secrets, left apart. The sound
of your galoshes clomping off hung
like tar in the overcast air.
I stood for a moment beneath the green
marquee, the entrance light splitting
my shadow over a slanted pole. Half of me
shrank from the short-lived laughter
we shared while we were strangers. Half
clung to what was no longer there.

Reciprocity

She has been fighting the same
battle all her life.
      Only now
the crisis seems feigned,
    the hurt old.

  You've heard her go on
too many times, even
  supplied ammo for the cause,
       fuel for the holidays.

Not much
  at stake these days.
No highs, no lows.
   Nothing to speak
 of, really. What was once
a forest is now a field. Stay in touch?
    Why that's understood with a click and steady tone.

Better a dreary photograph,
or limp refrain
    than never
a flash or jingle. A rumor, news
of a divorce: you would have offered more
than that. We left each other
to age, grow tired, bore the world,
you once confessed.
      How to hang up
       the phone
     without feeling hard,
      unfeeling.

Against Wasps

I

They must have been
at it all summer: securing a stay
for winter. Strange I didn't notice
   until now.
               In and out—they zoom
through the crevice between the brick
and wood, on the underside
of the eaves.
              The leaves
are falling. I don't want to kill
them, destroy what
they've done. They are
too many.

II

Building a colony
is not a spoon of honey,
and to buzz and sting must not
   be easy either.
              I don't want
to destroy what they've done. How can I
kill them? They are too many. The leaves
are falling.
           Dusk is the best time,
advises the man at the hardware
store. If only I could see
their work, maybe I could learn
something and we could go
on sharing this shelter.

III

No, I must kill them. The leaves
are falling. I can't see
what they've done. They are
   too many.
            Come sundown,
the work has halted. I stand
six feet away, aim,
unload the spray. A jet
of poison tears the air
and floods their entrance-
way.
    A few wasps,
trying to escape, fall
to the ground. Then nothing
except my heart
in my throat, some crickets,
a small wind in the trees.

IV

The next morning
the wasps are back
at work—buzzing on,
   busier than ever.
            Their nest
was too far to reach, too deep
in the cleft. They buzz on
as if my failed attempt
only strengthened
their mission, empowered
their queen.
        They were too many.
I'll never know what they've done. I tried
to kill them while the leaves
were falling. They don't care
what I've done.

Clawing at Bark

I *Tigris Balica*

The men who killed you
didn't fear the waringin tree,

never clawed the bark, lurked
near the river. They came

with guns not hunger. They never
knew your stripes, the stealth

of the stalk, how amid
the rushing pounce—all jugular,

all jaw—you were born
again. Caught in the crosshairs

of myth's immolation, where could you
turn but to the trees, to the tall leaves

quivering? Bullet beats fear beats flesh
beats breath. Where but to the sea?

Emperor of nightfall, great cat
gone to ghost, your lore

remains the lure, the scent
of loss in a fallen forest, the old bark

scabbing back its silence. How faithful
your eyes in the witching hour—

how sacred your blood.

II *Tigris Sondaica*

Your blood spilled in the witching hour.
Your light drowned in the moon.

Master of solitude, sentry
of seclusion, we lost another island—

we lost you. The wind
sent your mark to the temples,

to the mountains, back
to the waringin tree. You leapt

into bark, became the dusk
when the last of your kind

curled its claws and vanished.
Was that you tiger, when the sea

glinted twice, rose and went black?
Tiger, was that you carved

in the mist above the river?
Greed buries grief buries guilt buries blame.

Your pelt poached in the shadows.
Your bones sold in the sun.

Impudence precludes amnesty. The commerce
of disappearance sharpens the crime.

We will be forgotten like the dinosaurs.

III *Tigris Virgata*

They used steel traps
and strychnine, when they

cleared the forests. Charade
and cliché. Starved on the shores

of the Caspian Sea, you could
have torn them to pieces, plucked

flesh from bone, spit
their hearts out, had their eyes

met yours. Feline of calm,
king of enigma, when you roared

the wind held its breath
and became an altar. Your eyes

caught fire in the dusk, stripped
bark to pulp, devoured pain

until the tide tugged loose
and the moon was unnecessary.

Desertion betrays denouement betrays
descent betrays bereavement. Terrestrial

reprise. This world?
We too are passing through.

This world or the next?

Pinnacle

I've waited most of my life
for that mountain to crack,
to reverse into phantoms

that chase me. For a moment
to beckon the cloudburst, crush
the limitations, take hold

of the core. Possessed
by lightning, that rupture
would carry me across seasons—

through forests, surging
sands and soundless waters—
over so many footsteps

in the snow. I won't lose hold
of the ropes. Beyond the burnt
down bungalows of wanderers

who still sing to the haze, I'll
extol what flickers, all that
remains. On jagged cliffs of irony

and erosion, I'll wait
in the whisper for the falcon
to brand me with the edge of the sun.

Off Camera

Venetian Mask

Stare too long and the face
on the wall will tempt you, ask
for your eyes.
          For your eyes, take
my mouth, nose, lips, cheeks,
my Byzantine blush, take
my gilded braid. My bells. Hear?
Here are my bells.
            Transformed
in disguise, your eyes assume a chill
concealed, the face before the face,
only your eyes.
          Lend me your cape,
you implore, a three cornered
hat, the silk hood of night. Made
immortal, you travel to Carnival
with lips that neither smile
nor frown. There you seek
the true face of your mask, the hands
that first lifted your papier-
mâché.
       Do you know who I am?
you ask who you were. I rewrote
the story of Genesis on the narthex. I gave
Constantinople back his four bronze
horses. I climbed the tower
and rang the five iron
bells:
     Marangona, Maleficio, Nona,
Trottiera, Pregadi.
              We wandered
the Grand Canal in the sunset
       of a city slowly sinking.

Millennium Retribution in Key West

I

Ten centuries in the ricochet,
      a speck in the hourglass,
            dot of rain,
         retread,
          void.

We deserve this failure. Nothing stopped.
    What was is
        what is
           is what
               will be.

II

Damp first light, small
      through the blinds.
          Paper hats,
      half empty tumblers,
        discarded whistles,
           horns.

The world did not end. Nothing is not now
        how it's always
      been. Time, even in our
    time, is not our
      measure.

III

Nothing ticking
   except the memory
of Mallory Square: drinks
   on the wharf,
          the circus
speeding up—jugglers, ropewalkers, boats
casting off, gulls on the surge, salt on the gulp,
          the Gulf,
a turquoise window, a sunset tequila. Toss it back—
   some of the best moments
begin without caring
          —bite into the lemon.

IV

What novelty in sameness.
   How many others have come
hoping to dance,
          searching
for a vein to place their fingers on?
   A fresh glimpse
     at the continuum?
          Emptiness too
is a kind of fullness. The night gave
   more than it took. Soon I will head north
and see frost on the grass.
          Knowing nothing,
   I'll know nothing is missing.

Consolation

The chalked blue is electric
and keeps him reaching:
melting his focus, blazing his blur.
He grips the iron poker, ponders
murder, then turns the lit log.

It was easy to snap the brushwood,
stroke the matches, watch things
grow. But after he stains his shirt
sweeping up the ash, he knows
shooting sparks are unlike stars

or rebellion. The fire he built
for the first time did not die
from neglect, his watered eyes,
or because the steadiness of the blue
flame finally faltered. The wood

had nothing more to give is all. It's not
as if the ash could recall the flame,
or he could trail the smoke all the way
to the grave. Not as if the world
he built was magic or could burn a paler blue.

Nocturne with a Dash of Oblivion

What surrenders to night unleashes night:

The dryness in your throat, a scratch, daggers
of silicon, footsteps in a dream, a figure, untraceable,
but there beneath a brave hammock of stars,
the pumpkin moon close enough to carve, the figure—
there again, but too far
                —a ninja known only to night.

What listens to night belongs to night:

To air, leaves, cold, silence
through the hills. To the spider weaving
silk like fingers on Braille. To the cat
by the window—rapt in the lookout, burned
into darkness
            —watching the staked fields wait for the soldiers.

Third Law of Moxie

I

It is the day after winter
carnival and the vagrants
are playing chess in the park
again.
      The sky
anchors in fog. I stand
near an empty fountain waiting
for your arrival. Pigeons peck
around trash bins. Workers
dismantle a kiosk. Hands
in jacket, I wait for the sun
to burn through. Knight
takes rook.
           The workers laugh.

II

When you arrived, the sun
was in hiding. When you told me
it was over, I clenched
my pockets. You wore pink
mittens.
       I reached to touch you,
you turned away. The fountain
was empty. The carnival
had passed. Your eyes
were distraught. The sky
was at anchor. Your resolve
sped north on a train. Workers
hammered. Pigeons
wobbled. I reached,
you turned.
        North,
but two towns behind
schedule. The vagrants studied

the board, the passed pawn,
the queen. The way you moved
tasted like theft, like salt, like taffy,
the way your mittens caught
your eyes, the way
you looked back through
the fog forged me to snow
as the hammer fell
silent.

III

I will go south. Not for
the winter. For a spurting
fountain, a little
sun. You will write a letter
in lovely cursive. The vagrants
will remain in endgame until the carnival
returns. Stay strong,
you'll say. Take care
of yourself.
    Strong?
Pieces of you are still moving
through me. The sky
won't set sail. The workers
won't whistle. And who
will take care
of the pigeons? The king
in perpetual check? Your
mittens?
  You too,
I'll echo, as though those
wooden syllables—the first planks
of parting—could
somehow dignify another point of tangency.

Moratorium

The snow had fallen
without mystery: the last
of a season.
         We sprawled
around the fire sipping bourbon,
the first of a bottle.
               What was Theodor Geisel's middle name?
The pursuit felt more
trivial than an orange wedge
or another
        turn, but the question
lingered like a melody.
                Earlier, we'd zig-
                    zagged
                down slopes
             at great speeds,
          laughed in the face
         of danger, frost
        on the nose,
         numb toes. Now we were marshmallows:
veritable toads.
   Someone should
know this, said someone
who already knew.
             But knowledge
was harder to summon in the mountains,
with the weather so close
and furtive; it froze much faster than action
or pause.
       Far too safe
to be sure, no one
on our team knew
for sure. Outside, the trees
slumped   forward
      under wet clumps of snow.

                        The answer was read:
the game brought to an end.
I tossed back my drink and stared at the flames.
    When I awoke,
                it was snowing again
and everyone had gone to bed.
                        The last of the fire hissed blue
and under the outdoor lights,
   the falling flakes looked brighter and bigger
      than even us
                gliding through.
Tomorrow we would leave the whiteness,
      come
           down
        from the mountains,
                drift away
             to nothing new.
                        As the fire faded, the cadence
                             of the snow
                                  drew closer.
It was then I first knew
                the magic of stillness,
             why we had given up on the game,
                why Seuss persisted
                     and why
                —not here or there,
not even anywhere—
   he would have refused to like those slopes.

Snow & Branches

for Madeleine

Born to be born in winter, the last to be born,
you grew up too soon. Your father died before

you knew your father, starkness and slow
down, the bolt on the door. You knew all along

how to snub the cold, get by in the dark.
Buried in yourself, you were not as others were,

sweet secret. Mending, in your diary, melted
innocence. Truth muffled fact. Did your music

find meaning in the branches? What did you
cling to—if in your dreams you were snow—

who did you forgive? The years hang like icicles
from a roof memory can't yet sun to water.

Potomac at Last Light First

Take this nation, the setting sun, that 555-foot
obelisk across the river. Steady your finger
in front of your nose. Narrow your eyes.

Replace it. Now your hand. The sun. This nation.

While you're at it, pluck up that Parthenon, too. (Careful
with those 36 Doric columns.) Tuck it in your pocket.

Slip away unseen. Steady ... cling to what you can until dawn—

until the light blushes crimson over the ripples,
    shorebirds tent themselves in flight,
        until the willows weep, until they fan
            their shadows, drink
                      tears along the banks:

along this dreamy, snaky parkway zooming by—
      remake what you have taken.
                    Retrace it.

Espresso at Villa Cimbrone

Vaulted cloisters in morning light

Labyrinth of umbrella pines: the fragrant dare of early June
Suspended belvedere: the Gulf of Salerno,
Its courtly brew, brackish breeze through trellised wisteria

Sketching the wind
Painting the sky's breath
On water

Such dreams ... such impossible waking

He leans against the parapet
She bends to pink camellia

When sun takes the cliffs, reflex slips to tide,
Vista to vista, wave on wave, what statues

Over majolica floors
Under frescoed ceilings
They gesture through halls.

Raking Leaves

In the fading light you comb back
and forth the whole of your life.

Under the dogwoods you gather
the seeds and kindling of childhood.

A maple in the wind sprinkles
adolescence with copper confetti.

And by the birches the bark ages
and peels you away. Why is it

the oak offers the acorn you know
by heart? The past inside a shell

of incompletion? You knew that
by heart once too, before you understood

the pattern of the leaves: the future—the nip
of the season, now the dusk—you see

but haven't raked through yet.

As Twilight Winks

alone ashore at eventide
each wave
breaks back

today

a gull
spread against
the heliotrope sky

won't change
what it is

today

dies
without apology

I'll never know
what it was

ashore alone
the surf is painting
all I might have done

had I been
alone ashore
before

today

began
I could've swam
above taupe sea stars

dried
in breaking light

today

would've been divine
without me

with all
that goes unnoticed
tacked on its tide

of all things one
could do with it

where it begins
how to find

today

each jibe seeks harbor
in the drowned pendulum
prepared to come about

I'll miss how its slow
going grows how

today

couldn't help but go
where it's going
is not what it is

bow to advent
stern to valediction
below the edge of light

a day

winks softly and hides
alone so sure this eventide

Off Camera

Going, all but gone,
starting off slowly to name what had been,
the far-flung thunder, the empty house
became a character
of its own. Became the wet
wind against the windows,
a small tree bent backwards
towards the street, its leaves
all but gone. Not gone yet, but going.

I peered from the curtains,
the steps, through the eyes
of a Rembrandt, an attitude of clay.

She held the cup to her lips, but did not drink.

Does living out your part, does
wearing the future like a spray of jasmine and almond
make the action any more memorable?

She led him upstairs, her black silk
scarf bouncing softly about her bare shoulders.

There is an audience
for the applause you refuse. There is a proscenium
you burnt to ashes long ago.

She undressed gracefully and moved towards the bed.

All but gone, going. What had begun
so casually in the tied down corners of the stage
in the end began to carol.

Started off ... all but—
you must've been beautiful in your sadness,
must've been brilliant the days you sulked between the lines.
Come closer, she said. Come show me who I was.